CIRCUS
HIDDEN PICTURES

Selected by Jody Taylor

Boyds Mills Press

COVER

Bring on the Clowns!

So much fun going on at once! As the clowns and animals do their tricks, see if you can find sixteen objects hidden in the picture. Look for a crown, shovel, knitted hat, scoop, mushroom, hairbrush, baby's rattle, wedge of cheese, wishbone, rabbit's head, broom, horse, artist's paintbrush, slice of lemon, bird, and a piece of cake.

Copyright © 1994 by Boyds Mills Press
All rights reserved

Published by Bell Books
Boyds Mills Press, Inc.
A Highlights Company
815 Church Street
Honesdale, Pennsylvania 18431
Printed in the United States of America

Publisher Cataloging-in-Publication Data
Main entry under title :
    Circus hidden pictures / selected by Jody Taylor.—1st ed.
[32]p. : ill. ; cm.
Summary : Various objects are hidden in illustrations of circus scenes.
ISBN 1-56397-358-8
1. Puzzles—Juvenile literature. [1. Picture puzzles.] I. Taylor, Jody.
II. Title.
793.73—dc20   1994   CIP
Library of Congress Catalog Card Number 93-72919   AC

First edition, 1994
Book designed by Tim Gillner
The text of this book is set in 10-point Clarendon Light.

10 9 8 7 6 5 4 3 2

Clown Capers

J. J. and Jo Jo make everyone laugh as they pretend to row away in a teacup. But what is J. J. looking for with that telescope? Could it be the hidden football, penguin, sock, rabbit, glass, butterfly, dolphin, pliers, mouse, toothbrush, owl, and musical notes?

Coco in the Center Ring

The audience cheers when Coco the clown balances on the horse's back. As she goes round and round the ring, see if you can find a rabbit's head, broom, pine tree, banana, cat's head, crescent moon, dolphin, high-heeled boot, spoon, lizard, star, snake, candy cane, bird, and a spider.

Dog Parade

The performing dogs strut down the street to announce the arrival of the circus. While the band plays on, try to find the sock, spoon, bird, mitten, hairbrush, broom, purse, light bulb, sailboat, open book, baseball, carrot, fish, and the duck.

The Circus Is Coming!

Almost every boy and girl in town has seen one of these posters. But did they notice fifteen things hidden in the picture? Where are the ice-cream cone, goose's head, bell, pipe, baseball, T-shirt, pair of pants, golf club, mushroom, bone, kite, apple, baseball bat, elephant's head, and the piece of rope?

Performing Horses

Listen to the applause as the Amazing Wonder Horses spin, walk on their hind legs, and bow. Before they leave the center ring, see if you can find a hidden candle, fish, carrot, spoon, light bulb, rabbit, ice-cream cone, eyeglasses, spool of thread, sock, goose, sailboat, pot, clothespin, and cat.

Clowns to the Rescue

A clown's job is never done, and that's especially true at the circus. The Blooper Brothers may save the cat and put out the fire, but will they have time to collect a frying pan, key, wrench, mug, bell, mallet, screwdriver, magnifying glass, book, half an apple, pencil, and a hairbrush?

Circus History

In the early 1900s small circuses like this one traveled from town to town to put on shows in the summer. Boys and girls were so excited to be this close to the animals that they didn't notice the hidden hammer, eel, vase, fork, ladle, fish, bird, man's face, coffee pot, owl, pair of pants, pig's head, and turtle.

Fun on the Midway

Before the circus show begins, Tony and Josh want to try some of the rides and win a few prizes. You can join in the fun by finding seventeen hidden items: a ruler, duck, hat, dog, snowman, glove, sneaker, bear, watermelon, hot dog, sailboat, mushroom, cap, slipper, brush, sock, and a picture of Christopher Columbus.

Runaway Circus Act

Uh-oh! Maybe Clyde the clown shouldn't have taught the animals how to ride the bicycle and skateboard. Look at all the hidden objects scattered along the way. Will you help pick up the worm, carrot, mushroom, wristwatch, seal, boot, key, deer's head, canoe, open book, ring, bee, nail, and the ice-cream cone?

Moving Day

It's time for the circus to pack up and move on to the next town. The clowns really want to help, but they've misplaced so many things. Can you help them find a safety pin, magnet, screwdriver, hammer, ice skate, ring, lock, key, sunglasses, bottle, open book, bracelet, anchor, sailboat, candy cane, mailbox,

star, wristwatch, camera, ice-cream cone, lollipop, light bulb, paper clip, tree, table, feather duster, flag, pretzel, box of popcorn, jug, can, glass, fishing pole, spatula, recorder, and an egg holder?

Toby Joins the Circus

It looks as if the clowns have a new partner in the act. Once Toby learns how to jump through the hoop, maybe he can fetch the hidden radish, funnel, light bulb, shovel, musical note, key, spoon, mallet, toothbrush, bell, ladle, and feather.

First Carousel Ride

Mindy's younger brother is enjoying his first carousel ride so much he doesn't want to get off. As he keeps on going around and around, help Mindy find twenty hidden objects: a candy cane, cowboy hat, mop, penguin, ship, button, coffee pot, iron, stocking hat, sock, bottle, duck's head, vase, comb, shoe, sombrero, doughnut, lollipop, banana, and a fish.

The Clown Express

The audience always cheers when the Clown Express chugs and toots around the ring. When the smoke clears, see if you can locate a hidden butterfly, mouse, telephone receiver, tea kettle, doughnut, dog, egg, spool of thread, derby hat, horseshoe, thimble, rabbit, and pumpkin.

16

High-Wire Walkers

While all eyes are on the Seven Santinis and their amazing balancing act, try to find thirteen items hidden around the acrobats. Where are the cup, sewing needle, golf club, pine tree, sailboat, crayon, piece of pie, butterfly, acorn, dog, ax, bird, and the letter **A**?

Circus Animals on the Loose!

This backyard ringmaster will have to catch his circus performers before the show can begin. While he's out collecting his "wild animals," see if you can find a pushpin, candle, mitten, artist's paintbrush, closed umbrella, shovel, flashlight, sewing needle, screw, banana, pencil, and a piece of pie.

Talented Trio

Whenever the Barnaby Brothers perform, the center ring is filled with juggling balls, bubbles, and balloons. But today there are eighteen other things filling the center ring as well. How long will it take you to find a bowl, banana, sailboat, candle, button, snowman, sausage, comb, pitcher, mushroom, snail, sweater, cat's head, ice skate, ladder, wedge of cheese, strawberry, and a toothbrush?

The Animals' Circus

The big tent is finally set up, and it's time for the animals to rehearse their acts. In all the noisy fun and confusion, can you find the hidden nail, bow, carrot, sailboat, magnifying glass, fish, record, hammer,

artist's paintbrush, seal, two combs, toothbrush, fork, rabbit, bell, snake, pear, spoon, bowl, paper clip, iron, safety pin, mouse, and two frogs?

Under the Big Top

The center ring is filled with action, excitement, and hidden objects. Do you see a hammer, pencil, goose, archery bow, piece of pie, hairbrush, crescent moon, fish, hat, banana, snake, and a bird's head?

Circus on Birch Street

Amy and Mark are just about ready to put on a circus show for everyone in the neighborhood. They're too busy to look for hidden items now, so you will have to find a snake, toothbrush, shovel, fish, butterfly, ice-cream cone, pencil, cat, rabbit, bird, ladle, snail, hot dog, seal, and a funnel.

Circus Celebrities

These well-trained animals deserve to be the stars of the show. While they perform, see if you can locate the hidden sailboat, feather, eagle's head, snake, bird, chicken, spoon, caterpillar, woodpecker's head, and mouse.

Clowning Around

Even after the show, the clowns are up to more high jinks. They've hidden eleven things for you to find. Where are the sailboat, heart, sock, fish, horseshoe, saddle, mushroom, ram's head, cowboy hat, bird's head, and the letter **M**?

Up, Up, and Away!

Before the ringmaster discovers that the monkeys are taking a hot-air balloon ride, see if you can locate a light bulb, toothbrush, book, sewing needle, radish, pushpin, ice-cream cone, key, pliers, closed

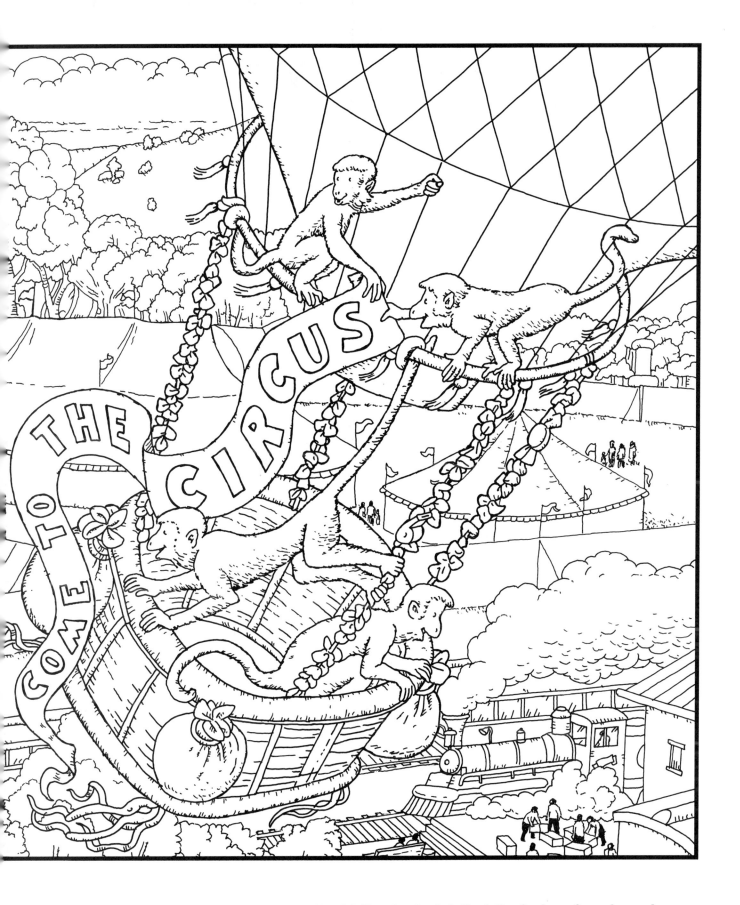

umbrella, piece of pie, crayon, wishbone, pencil, whistle, pinwheel, bell, stalk of celery, funnel, eyeglasses, paintbrush, bicycle tire pump, wrapped piece of candy, tack, and a tube of toothpaste.

Backyard Circus

Beth and her friends are putting on a great show to make money for the animal shelter. But how did all those hidden objects get into the act? Before the show is over, try to find a comb, pencil, cup, drinking straw, whale, bird, bottle, slice of bread, coin, gorilla's head, paintbrush, record, candle, adhesive bandage, and a spool of thread.

ANSWERS

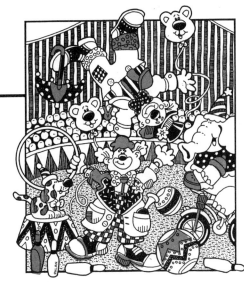

Cover: crown, shovel, knitted hat, scoop, mushroom, hairbrush, baby's rattle, wedge of cheese, wishbone, rabbit's head, broom, horse, artist's paintbrush, slice of lemon, bird, piece of cake

3: football, penguin, sock, rabbit, glass, butterfly, dolphin, pliers, mouse, toothbrush, owl, musical notes

4: rabbit's head, broom, pine tree, banana, cat's head, crescent moon, dolphin, high-heeled boot, spoon, lizard, star, snake, candy cane, bird, spider

5: sock, spoon, bird, mitten, hairbrush, broom, purse, light bulb, sailboat, open book, baseball, carrot, fish, duck

6: ice-cream cone, goose's head, bell, pipe, baseball, T-shirt, pair of pants, golf club, mushroom, bone, kite, apple, baseball bat, elephant's head, piece of rope

7: candle, fish, carrot, spoon, light bulb, rabbit, ice-cream cone, eyeglasses, spool of thread, sock, goose, sailboat, pot, clothespin, cat

8: frying pan, key, wrench, mug, bell, mallet, screwdriver, magnifying glass, book, half an apple, pencil, hairbrush

9: hammer, eel, vase, fork, ladle, fish, bird, man's face, coffee pot, owl, pair of pants, pig's head, turtle

10: ruler, duck, hat, dog, snowman, glove, sneaker, bear, watermelon, hot dog, sailboat, mushroom, cap, slipper, brush, sock, picture of Christopher Columbus

11: worm, carrot, mushroom, wristwatch, seal, boot, key, deer's head, canoe, open book, ring, bee, nail, ice-cream cone

12-13: safety pin, magnet, screwdriver, hammer, ice skate, ring, lock, key, sunglasses, bottle, open book, bracelet, anchor, sailboat, candy cane, mailbox, star, wristwatch, camera, ice-cream cone, lollipop, light bulb, paper clip, tree, table, feather duster, flag, pretzel, box of popcorn, jug, can, glass, fishing pole, spatula, recorder, egg holder

14: radish, funnel, light bulb, shovel, musical note, key, spoon, mallet, toothbrush, bell, ladle, feather

15: candy cane, cowboy hat, mop, penguin, ship, button, coffee pot, iron, stocking hat, sock, bottle, duck's head, vase, comb, shoe, sombrero, doughnut, lollipop, banana, fish

16: butterfly, mouse, telephone receiver, tea kettle, doughnut, dog, egg, spool of thread, derby hat, horseshoe, thimble, rabbit, pumpkin

17: cup, sewing needle, golf club, pine tree, sailboat, crayon, piece of pie, butterfly, acorn, dog, ax, bird, letter **A**

18: pushpin, candle, mitten, artist's paintbrush, closed umbrella, shovel, flashlight, sewing needle, screw, banana, pencil, piece of pie

19: bowl, banana, sailboat, candle, button, snowman, sausage, comb, pitcher, mushroom, snail, sweater, cat's head, ice skate, ladder, wedge of cheese, strawberry, toothbrush

20-21: nail, bow, carrot, sailboat, magnifying glass, fish, record, hammer, artist's paintbrush, seal, two combs, toothbrush, fork, rabbit, bell, snake, pear, spoon, bowl, paper clip, iron, safety pin, mouse, two frogs

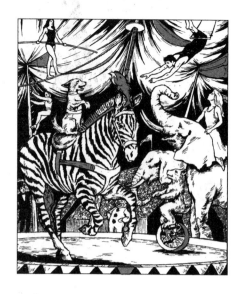

22: hammer, pencil, goose, archery bow, piece of pie, hairbrush, crescent moon, fish, hat, banana, snake, bird's head

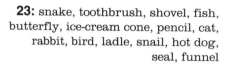

23: snake, toothbrush, shovel, fish, butterfly, ice-cream cone, pencil, cat, rabbit, bird, ladle, snail, hot dog, seal, funnel

24: sailboat, feather, eagle's head, snake, bird, chicken, spoon, caterpillar, woodpecker's head, mouse

25: sailboat, heart, sock, fish, horseshoe, saddle, mushroom, ram's head, cowboy hat, bird's head, letter **M**

26-27: light bulb, toothbrush, book, sewing needle, radish, pushpin, ice-cream cone, key, pliers, closed umbrella, piece of pie, crayon, wishbone, pencil, whistle, pinwheel, bell, stalk of celery, funnel, eyeglasses, paintbrush, bicycle tire pump, wrapped piece of candy, tack, tube of toothpaste

28: comb, pencil, cup, drinking straw, whale, bird, bottle, slice of bread, coin, gorilla's head, paintbrush, record, candle, adhesive bandage, spool of thread